HERBS

Flowers

Bees Buzzz

Flowers

For Love of the

GARDEN

For
Kathy
who brought
sunshine to my
life! Dianne

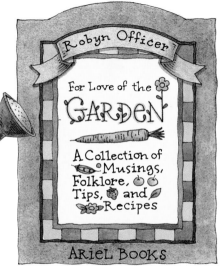

Robyn Officer

For Love of the
GARDEN

A Collection of
Musings,
Folklore,
Tips, and
Recipes

ARIEL BOOKS

**Andrews McMeel
Publishing**

Kansas City

For Love of the Garden: A Collection of Musings, Folklore, Tips, and Recipes

 For information write Andrews McMeel Publishing, an Andrews McMeel Universal company, 4520 Main Street, Kansas City, Missouri 64111.

ISBN: 0-7407-1432-5
Library of Congress Catalog Card Number: 00-106940

This book is dedicated
to all those who
have toiled in
and
loved a garden.

R.O.

Whether you are feeling the dirt between your fingers or standing back to admire the delicate beauty of your handiwork, your garden is a source of strength and pride. Filled with herbs, vegetables, or blossoms, your garden of plenty can bring endless joy to you and others.

Welcome to my GARDEN

Gardens refresh your emotions and cleanse your spirit. They are especially rewarding because no two are alike. You decide what goes in and what comes out; flowers or fruit— it's up to you.

This little book contains charming artwork along-side thoughtful quotations, advice, folk wisdom, and recipes. Read and celebrate your love for *your* garden and all that it gives back to you each year.

I ♥ my garden

Life begins
the day you start
a garden.

—Chinese proverb

More
than anything,
I must have
flowers,
always, always.

Claude Monet

O, what delights to us the garden ground doth bring? Seed, leaf, flower, fruit, herb, bee, and tree, and more than I may sing.

—Nicholas Grimaed

To dig and delve in nice clean dirt can do a mortal little hurt.

—John Kendrick Bangs

Radishes

pulled up as
the Moon wanes
will cure corns
& warts.

The cottage garden is lavish with brilliant flowers of all shapes and sizes lining walkways, hanging from trellises, and climbing walls. It is a seemingly hodgepodge arrangement of nature running rampant, but with a carefully executed design.

Earth
laughs in
flowers.

—Ralph Waldo Emerson

ASTER – loyalty

ROSE – love

IRIS – dashed hopes

NARCISSUS – vanity

Pick flowers early in the morning, before the sun has a chance to sap their strength.

Flowers are the sweetest things God ever made and forgot to put a soul into.

—Henry Ward Beecher

CARNATION-steadfastness

LILAC-young love

VIOLET-modesty

SUNFLOWER-happiness

NASTURTIUM-lost love

When in these fresh mornings
I go into my garden before
anyone is awake, I go for
the time being into perfect
happiness. In this hour
divinely fresh
and still,

the fair face of every flower salutes me with a silent joy that fills me with infinite content; each gives me its color, its grace, its perfume, and enriches me with the consummation of its beauty.

—Celia Thaxter

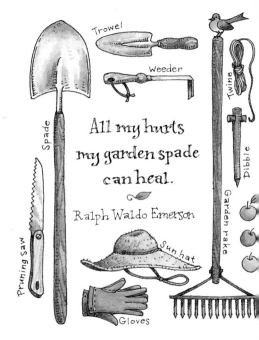

All my hurts
my garden spade
can heal.

Ralph Waldo Emerson

Trowel

Weeder

Spade

Twine

Dibble

Garden rake

Pruning Saw

Sun hat

Gloves

Yes, in the poor man's garden grow

Far more than herbs and flowers —

Kind thoughts, contentment, peace

of mind, And joy for weary hours.
—Mary Howitt

There is
more pleasure
in making a
garden
than in
contemplating
a paradise.

—Anne Scott-James

To own a bit of ground,
to scratch it with a hoe,
to plant seeds and
watch the renewal
of life —
this is the common-
est delight of the
race, the most
satisfactory thing a
man can do.

—Charles Dudley Warner

The Rose Garden

- The rose reigns as the queen of flowers, prized for its transcendent beauty as well as its exquisite scent.

- Attar of roses is oil distilled from rose flowers and is used as a basis for perfumes. Five thousand pounds of fresh rose petals are necessary to make one pound of attar!

THERE SHOULD
BE BEDS of ROSES,
BANKS of ROSES,
BOWERS of ROSES,
EDGINGS of ROSES,
BASKETS of ROSES,
VISTAS and ALLEYS
of ROSES.

Reverend Samuel Reynolds Hole

Making...
Rose Water:

Steep rose petals in a glass bowl of warm water until they lose their color. Then strain the water and repeat the procedure until you're satisfied with the intensity of the scent. Place in a glass bottle and refrigerate until use.

Robert Herrick • dying. •

ye may, Old time is still a-flying; And this same

Musk rose

Floribunda

Noisette

Hybrid tea

Polyantha

Roses

Rose hip

Damask

English rose

flower that smiles to

HERE AT MY FEET WHAT
WONDERS PASS, WHAT ENDLESS,
ACTIVE LIFE IS HERE! WHAT
BLOWING DAISIES, FRAGRANT GRASS!
—Matthew Arnold

What a man needs in gardening is a cast-iron back with a hinge on it.

—Charles Dudley Warner

Bees are not as busy.

I planted there a
whisp of feathery
grey,
And waited, seven
years of nights
and days;
And now before my
door there shining
stands
A bee cathedral,
thunderous with
praise.

—Fenella Boyle

as we think they are. They just can't buzz any slower.

—Kin Hubbard

Buzzz

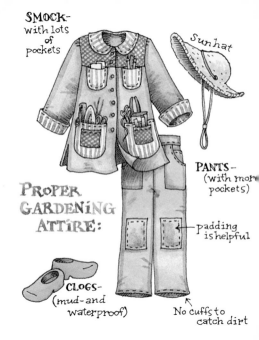

SMOCK-
with lots
of
pockets

Sunhat

PANTS-
(with more
pockets)

PROPER GARDENING ATTIRE:

padding
is helpful

CLOGS-
(mud- and
waterproof)

No cuffs to
catch dirt

Black thread tied around fruit bushes will protect them from birds.

THE
SPRING GARDEN

Spring has come when you can put your foot on three daisies.

—Traditional folk wisdom

Daffodil

Crocus

SOME
SPRING-BLOOMING
BULBS:

Each spring... a garden-
ing instinct, sure as the
sap rising in the trees,
stirs within us. We look
about and decide to
tame another little bit
of ground.

—Lewis Gannett

Hyacinth

Snowdrop

Tulip

Muscari

HOW TO BUY BULBS:

Healthy bulbs, like healthy gardeners, are firm, unshriveled, and have no soft spots.

NATURALIZING with BULBS:

Some bulbs, such as crocuses and narcissi, often look more attractive naturalized in a lawn or meadow than planted in an ornamental bed. A good way to naturalize these bulbs is to scatter by hand and then plant them where they land.

Daffodils,
That come before the
    swallow dares, and take
The winds of March
    with beauty.

—William Shakespeare

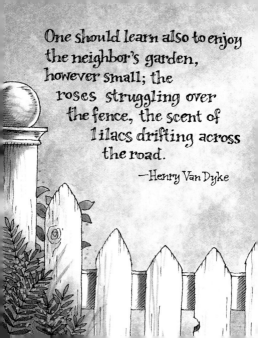

One should learn also to enjoy the neighbor's garden, however small; the roses struggling over the fence, the scent of lilacs drifting across the road.

—Henry Van Dyke

A good gardener always plants three seeds—

one for the grubs,

one for the weather,

one for himself.

—C. Collins

There is life in the ground: It goes into the seeds, and it also,

when it is stirred up, goes into the man who stirs it.

—Charles Dudley Warner

GARDEN FRIENDS

The kiss of the sun
for pardon,
The song of the birds
for mirth,
One is nearer God'
heart in a garden
Than anywhere else
on earth.

—Dorothy Frances Gurney

PLANTS THAT ATTRACT HUMMINGBIRDS:

Bee balm · Columbine · Penstemon ·
Four-o'clock · Honeysuckle ·
Hollyhock · Trumpet creeper

PLANTS THAT ATTRACT BUTTERFLIES:

Aster · Coreopsis · Dianthus ·
Sweet William · Zinnia ·
Phlox · Butterfly weed · Cosmos

American settlers in the 1800s planted giant sunflowers around their houses in the belief that they would protect them from malaria.

My Garden
Will Never Make
Me Famous,
I'm A
Horticultural
Ignoramus.

—Ogden Nash

THE Kitchen GARDEN

A kitchen garden should be located just a few steps outside the kitchen door, in a sunny spot where a cook can easily pluck a few fresh herbs or a handful of tender leaves for a salad.

When skies are blue
and days are bright
A kitchen-garden's my
delight,
Set round with rows
of decent box
And blowsy girls
of hollyhocks.

—Katharine Tynan

Some Edible Flowers:

Nasturtium
  (flowers & leaves)
Marigolds
Violets
Geraniums
Daisy petals
Cornflower
Lilacs
Rose petals
Honeysuckle
Bee balm

lovely

use as a garnish

decorate a tart

toss in a salad

a bit of color

In order to
live off a garden,
you practically
have to live
in it.

—Kin Hubbard

I don't know how people deal with their moods when they have no garden, raspberry patch, or field to work in. You can take your angers, frustrations, bewilderments to the earth, working savagely, working up a sweat and an ache and a great weariness. The work rinses

out the cup of your
spirit, leaves it washed
and clean and ready to
be freshly filled with
new hope. It is one of the
reasons I am addicted to
raspberry patches. The pie
is purely symbolic.

—Rachel Peden

Greenfly, it's difficult to see, Why

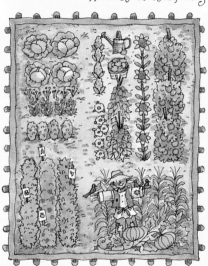

God, who made the rose, made thee.
— A.P. Herbert

On every stem, on every leaf, . . . and at the root of everything that grew, was a professional specialist in the shape of grub, caterpillar, aphis, or other expert, whose business it was to devour that particular part.

— Oliver Wendell Holmes

The HERB GARDEN

For romantics, herbs are some of nature's most charming creations. Their elegant demeanors, distinct fragrances, and delicious flavors, as well as their diverse benefits, lend them an almost magical quality.

Harvest herbs before they flower

HERBAL BATHS

After a long, hard day gardening, nothing beats a luxurious soak in the bathtub.

Toss herbs into the water or tie in cheesecloth, and let the herbs (and you) steep.

HERBAL VINEGAR

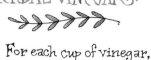

For each cup of vinegar, (red wine or white wine vinegar,) use three two-inch sprigs of herbs. Place the herbs in a glass jar. Then, heat the vinegar without boiling it, and pour it into the glass jar over the herbs. When it has cooled, cover the jar tightly and store in a cool, dark place.

As for rosemary,
I let it run all over my
garden walls
Not only because my bees
love it
But because 'tis the herb
Sacred to remembrance.

—Sir Thomas More

Rosmarinus officinalis

MINT – *Mentha*

Mint is said to cool tempers and take the heat off excessive emotions.

THYME – *Thymus vulgaris*

Because of its pungent, sweet scent, thyme is adored by bees. Thyme came to symbolize industrious activity.

NEVER ENOUGH THYME

SWEET BASIL
Ocimum basilicum

One of the great culinary herbs, basil is especially beloved in Italian cooking.

Basil stimulates the heart ♥ and relieves melancholy.

⁓ Herb Butter ⁓

Mix 1 or 2 tablespoons of chopped, fresh herbs (basil, tarragon, thyme, oregano) into half a cup of softened butter. Season with salt and pepper. Use on hot pasta or baste on grilled meats, vegetables, or fish.

Old gardeners never die. They just spade away and then throw in the trowel.

—Herbert V. Prochnow

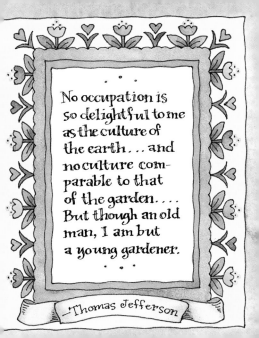

No occupation is so delightful to me as the culture of the earth . . . and no culture comparable to that of the garden. . . . But though an old man, I am but a young gardener.

—Thomas Jefferson

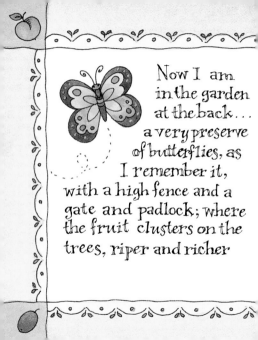

Now I am
in the garden
at the back...
a very preserve
of butterflies, as
I remember it,
with a high fence and a
gate and padlock; where
the fruit clusters on the
trees, riper and richer

than fruit has ever been since, in any other garden, and where my mother gathers some in a basket, while I stand by, bolting furtive gooseberries, and trying to look unmoved.

—Charles Dickens

A sure way to prevent mice from invading your garden is to wash your cat and sprinkle the water over your garden.

He who plants
a garden,
plants happiness.

Chinese proverb

The FRAGRANT GARDEN

Some Fragrant Blooms:

Lily of the valley · Lilac
Narcissus · Hyacinth · Rose
Iris · Honeysuckle · Pinks
Sweet pea · Jasmine
Daylily · Gardenia

The scents of plants
are like unseen ghosts.
They sneak upon you
as you round a turn
in the garden,
before you can see
the plants from
which they come.

—Barbara Damrosch

LAVENDER POTPOURRI

Gently mix the following in a ceramic or glass bowl:

1 oz. lavender
½ oz. wormwood
3 oz. thyme
1 tsp. crushed cloves
½ oz. rosemary

1 tsp. powdered orrisroot
¼ oz. mint
¼ oz. tansy

To make a lavender sachet...

Fill little cloth bags with potpourri and tie with a ribbon. Nestle the sachets among your lingerie or linens.

Tussie-Mussie

Scented nosegays, used in medieval times to mask unwanted odors.

The small bouquets were held to the nose when an offensive odor was detected

My friend first points out
on one side the beds of
basil, burnet, chives, but as
she turns to the other
side her eyes sparkle
with a happy light. For
this is her tussie-mussie
garden, mignonette, rosemary,
lemon verbena . . . all of
the old-time favorites. Each
plant is a personality,
each kind of herb a fragrant
memory for any visitor to
the garden.

—Rosetta E. Clarkson

Ever
since I could
remember anything,
flowers have been like
dear friends to me,
comforters,
inspirers,
powers to lift
and cheer.

Celia Thaxter

An old English legend has it that lily-of-the-valley blooms sprouted wherever drops of blood had fallen upon the ground from St. George, who had to battle a fierce, fire-breathing dragon.

I love to hear Real gardeners talking, the Latin names rolling off their tongue, sonorous and beautiful. I feel abashed when I take a sleeve and say, "Do come and see that pink thing over there."

"Ah, Centaurea hypoleuca.

"Very nice," they say.
Never mind. It smiles
the same for both of us.

—Pam Brown

Ranunculus gramineus

Campanula lactiflora

Dryopteris affinis

Penstemon

Viola

Gardening is a habit
of which I hope
never to be cured...

—Martha Smith